Davi Poems

Christian Poetry

DAVID LACHAPELLE

POEMS

The Bible

The Bible is a powerful book

There is no doubt

It cuts through the core of your soul

Like a two-edged sword

It can discern your thoughts

It can discern your intentions

It can guide your life

It is a tool to get by

It is a weapon

The more you read

The enemy is not pleased

Just trust in the Lord

The Bible is alive

It is God's word

To take you home

I Am a Believer

I lay down my life

To something greater in store

I see a higher calling

The world loses its color

There is more to this life

There is more than meets the eye

I am a believer

In the Lord

Jesus Christ

Potter and Clay

In this classroom of life

You are the potter

I am the clay

Shaping me

Every which way

Spin me round

I am dizzy

I am confused

I seek you

Stretch me forth

It hurts

Old me changed

I am new in you

Potter and Clay

Bake me in the oven

It is hot

I cannot breathe

Solidified in Christ

I am a trophy of his grace

To be one with the Lord

What he made of me

For eternity

Pride

Pride is everywhere

I am fighting against it

Not knowingly

It seeps in so slowly

I do not resist

I cannot insist

I can come to you

Oh Lord

To restore my peace

And remove my shame

And deliver me

From pride

Humility

Trust

The world is too big too navigate

Without having a compass to trust

In something beyond myself

Stretches me out of my comfort zone

To place me back to where I belong

Trust is something

You develop

Until it becomes a part of your life

Because he is dependable

Taking each day as it comes

Trust

Letting Go

I give up control

To know what is in store

I have no clue

I just think I do

Thoughts dissipate

The more I see you

And what you are up to

Your timing is perfect

You have me in

The palm of your hands

Giving me freedom

To cast my cares

To the one who created it all

Things are getting easier

I am letting go

Moving Forward

You are never in a hurry

You are always on time

You are never late

You show up

When I give up

Until the work is done in me

Moving on to

Greater challenges

To stretch my faith

And give me something

To celebrate

I am moving forward

Coming Around

You are the way

To guide me today

I am still in your loving arms

Knowing you are in control

I give up care to understand

There is less of me and more of you

Things are clearer

Now I can see

The things around me

Are orchestrated by you

Shaping my destiny

I see your face

In everything

I can relate

You won't disappoint

I am coming around

Leading Me

You are the light

You are the way

To brighten my day

To see what you are

And who I am meant to be

I do not know the future

But you do

I see your glory every step

That led me to this place

Of where I am now

It could not have been otherwise

For what you have in store

Surprise me

I am ready

A New Beginning

It is a new day

Who can say?

What is around the corner

I am ready to follow you

To be good to me

The war is over

End of myself

Liberated

From the struggles

Against all else

I surrender

Peace and comfort are my friends

I am whole and content

It is a new beginning

Rising

I forgive to be free

From bondage they do not see

He uses them against me

It hurts when they wound

Insult and injury

Have less effect

I am getting stronger

I am becoming whole

To see the purpose set before me

Being molded into Christ likeness

There is no place to run

I know their games

I rise above it all

Grateful

Trials and tribulations

Are my workout

For my spiritual muscles

To stretch my faith

And for my character development

To grow stronger in the Lord

Once upon a time

I wanted deliverance

Now I welcome my sufferings

with thanksgiving

so that I may

humble myself before you

and receive your power

from upon high

In this lowly position

Grateful

In this hour of need

You are my savior

I am grateful indeed

Temptation

I am tempted daily

I know the devil's tricks

I see his snares

An annoyance at best

If I am off balance

My guard comes up

To not think or do what is not me

Temptation

Waiting

I wait for you Lord

I do not know what for

Are you keeping score?

Changing me from the inside out

I am looking in the clouds

Whatever your will is

I trust you

Waiting is a hard classroom

Lessons learned

Ingrained in you

Take me to a new level

I am waiting

More to Life

When life's challenges confront

I turn to you

Oh Lord

I do not retaliate

And get caught up

In a cycle of hate

People are competing

I try to checkout

And seek you

To find out

Wisdom and maturity

I can be proud of

Turning to you

In every season

Leaves me wondering

There is more to life

More to Life

Then just believing

Liberty

I cast my cares

For everything will be ok

Trusting in the lord

God is in control

A new beginning

Let's see where it goes

He will return

Before you know

The planet shakes

Heaven waits

My only responsibility

Is humility

Nothing else matters

I can now see

Liberty

Eyes opened

Liberty

Anointed

Anoint me with oil

Burning so bright

Full of the holy spirit

Taking me closer to you

Changing the world

For your glory

Time will tell

The story reveals itself

Your life has meaning

If you would only look above

and see the temporal

nature of it all

That God's Kingdom

Is true purpose

I am anointed for this reason

I am anointed with oil

Anointed

for this season

Blessed

You test me

To see

If there is anything

that should not be

Ropes burned off

Chains broken

The heat

The pressure

Do not smell like smoke

I am not crushed

Refined and stirred

I am matured

To trust you

In everything I go through

To shape me for eternity

To a higher calling

Blessed

To walk with you

All these years

Who would have known?

It would have been like this

To come out of the furnace a trophy

I am blessed

Aware

Victory is making

The best of it

Where you are

And that is it

When you are locked in his grace

There maybe more

But who is to say?

And one day

See him face to face

Who knows the answers as to why?

Just to be aware

Fine

Restored

The negativity storm in my soul

Has been rescinded

Forevermore

The spirit to resist is gone

Left is open arms

To welcome the new

Lord I am humble

before you

That is all

I care about

Because I am

not in a drought anymore

I am restored

Right Standing

He hung on a tree

For you and me

To be one with God

To come boldly before the throne

To enter the holy gates

For the ones who will believe

In the name above all names

Jesus

Will be saved

On that special day

Empty Me

Full of myself
God has a plan
To show me
a better me

Had to unwind
To be kind
Come to the end
Of bondage within
The struggle was
limiting me
It is a process
to liberty
Empty me

Humble me

Knock me down again

Until I give up fighting

Have your way with me

I realize I am feeble and small

I need you for everything

Until I am nothing

Pride is the enemy

It is the cause

of all my troubles

I see its fleshly works

Creating separation

Empty me of me

Fill me with you

Until I can see

The beauty of it all

that is all around me to see

Humble me

Humble me

Amazed

Now I see

What you have been

trying to tell me

I learned more about you

In this exchange of me for you

Where I thought I would lose

I won

So strange

Yet perfect

In all his ways

I am amazed

The Furnace

The temperature is hot

I am suffocating

There is no way out

Must go through

The fiery trial that surrounds

What is there to learn

I am human

Burning off my limitations and pride

Imperfections refined

Wholeness is becoming

The person I am meant to be

The furnace purifies

Completely

Rescue

I trust you

When I do not know what to do

You are the light

When everything is not alright

You are the way

To direct my steps

You are my rock

I can lean on

You are the love

To comfort my soul

My saving Grace

That steady's the course

Through so much that is at my door

It is a lot to take in

You are my rescue

Victory

Victory is the Lords

I lay down my sword

He can fight better than me

He is more armed

and knows it all

I have courage

To let go

Into his loving arms

When the world

is falling all around

I see the good in life

I am the support

to lean on

because of his love

I shine the light

To show the way

Victory

To Victory

Hooray!

Won Over

I know where I am
Is for a reason
It just feels right
No matter the wrong
If I am supposed
to be somewhere else
I would be
Being content
where you are
It is how you get promoted

I am completely his
No longer my own
I have given over the key
To run my own life
I fought tooth and nail

Won Over

But his love prevailed

I thought by losing

I would be lost

But now I am found

And won over

Either Way

When things are looking great

I do not try to escape

Instead I run to him

Just like when I am under the gun

It is a different way

Trusting that God is on my side

Always

He wants me closer to him

To touch me with his grace

So that he may fill me up with his love

and bless me beyond

what I am capable of

Either way I am dependent

Gifted

I do not know anything

I am humble in my spirit

Just content to be no one

and rest in his love

to be fully surrendered

and be one with the Son

To trust in something higher

and not fight anymore

to have my way with the world

Dividing my soul

Struggles to be told

I am at the end

It is a new beginning

Everything is different

I am gifted

Always There

I trust in you

In everything I do

When the sun shines

When the clouds appear

When the rain falls

You are always there

To take me through

The narrow road to life

You do not change

I do not think twice

About your love

I hold near

You are my rock

You are always there

Diamond

Trials come and go

They are a steady press

To refine my soul

To be molded and shaped

It hurts to be pushed

Out of my comfort zone

I want it to end

I want it to be finished

I see the purpose

To make a diamond

out of coal

I can finally see

The brightness and beauty

Of my stone in other people's reflections

I am a diamond

Revelation

There is pride

All over the earth

It started with

Eve and the fruit of the tree

It has been hidden

Since the beginning of time

It is everywhere

Like a widespread disease

Now I see

Because God has revealed this to me

The element of pride

I did not see

That was unknown to me in me

Sanctified

I have come to the end of myself

I have nothing to give of me

I am all his

It is plain to see

I do not care

About this life

I am here

To be made right

In the sight of the Lord above

Sanctified

Holy

Ascension

Being molded and shaped
into something beautiful
to take into heaven
when I get there
Passing the tests
when they come
moves me forward
in my character development
to become the real-me
hiding nothing
showing his glory
to its fullness
is the purpose
behind it all
until we rise to his majesty
Ascension

Returning

What to do

But go to you

In your loving arms

Your warm embrace

You always take me back

When I have strayed

and been dismayed

You are my one true love

Holy and pure

I can count on

To save my soul

I am returning to you

Once and for all

Homeward Bound

It is a daily process

To give up the fight

To retain what is right

To unwind the self

To be able to let go

and be restored

To freedom's course

To see I do not have

To labor to complete me

Is total dependency

To the one who knows

To take you home

I am homeward bound

Jesus Is

I give all the glory to God

To know that Jesus is

my comforter

my counsellor

my teacher

my healer

my protector

my best friend

my master

And so much more

Showing me the way

He is everything I need

Forevermore

Made in the USA
Middletown, DE
25 January 2020